The Keys to

Daily Victory

SCRIPTURE KEYS
TO TAKE YOU FROM
STEP TO STEP

ROSEZETHA
JACKSON

The Keys to
Daily Victory

SCRIPTURE KEYS TO TAKE YOU
FROM STEP TO STEP

ROSEZETHA JACKSON

Cover Design by Erika Hollier, Interior Images by Rosezetha Jackson
Author photo by Tiffany Henny

Scripture quotations marked (KJV) are taken from the
KING JAMES VERSION and are available through the public domain.

Definitions quotations marked (WRUD) are taken from
Webster's Revised Unabridged Dictionary, © 2007, 2005
by Houghton Mifflin Harcourt Publishing Company. All rights reserved.
and Webster's New Pocket Dictionary, © 2007, 2005 by
Houghton Mifflin Harcourt Publishing Company. All rights reserved.

Main Page. (2022, October 5)
In Wikipedia. https://en.wikipedia.org/wiki/Main_Page

ISBN # 978-1-68593-121-6

Additional copies of this book are available from the Author
Rosezetha Jackson | rosezethajackson@gmail.com
Also Available on Amazon

WISE PUBLICATIONS
CUSTOM BOOK MANUFACTURING SINCE 1982
809 East Napoleon St., Sulphur, Louisiana 70663 | 337-527-8308
books@wisepublications.biz
Visit our online Bookstore! www.wisepublications.biz

The Keys to
Daily Victory

SCRIPTURE KEYS
TO TAKE YOU FROM
STEP TO STEP

This Book Is Dedicated To...

_____

THE ONE WHO TAUGHT ME THAT I AM:

"I will praise thee; for I am fearfully and wonderfully made marvelous
are thy works; and that my soul knoweth right well."
PS. 139:14 KJV

THE ONE WHO TAUGHT ME:

"And we know that all things work together for good
to them that love God, to them who are the called
according to his purpose."
RO. 8:28 KJV

THE ONE WHO TAUGHT ME:

"Let your conversation be without covetousness;
and be content with such things as ye have for he hath said,
I will never leave thee, nor forsake thee."
HE. 13:5 KJV

THE ONE WHO TAUGHT ME:

"For thy Maker is thine husband; the LORD of hosts
is his name; and thy Redeemer the Holy One of Israel;
The God of the whole earth shall he be called."
IS. 54:5 KJV

THE ONE WHO TAUGHT ME:

"Ye are of God, little children, and have overcome them: because
greater is he that is in you, than he that is in the world."
1 JN. 4:4 KJV

*This book is dedicated to the Lord Jesus Christ who suffered for me so
I can be who I am today. I humbly say thank you!*

I LOVE YOU MY HEAVENLY FATHER, ABBA!

Introduction

Are you willing to take the steps?

The answer to the question depends upon the determination of steps you take to get the victory over the obstacle/s, thing(s), or person(s) that is causing the hindrance in one's life. While going through life we will encounter different situations, but God gave us the keys in the word of God for our everyday situation(s) that we will encounter to overcome daily with victory. "And they overcame him by the blood of the lamb, and by the word of their testimony; and they loved not their lives unto the death." (Rev. 12:11 KJV) I want you to take the steps by faith to victory! We need these keys to assist us when communicating with God while praying for ourselves and others. The word of God tells us that; "Heaven and earth shall pass away, but my words shall not pass away." (Mt. 24:35 KJV, Mk. 13:31 KJV, Lu. 21:33 KJV)

*Remember this tool to overcome:

While going through situation(s) we have to believe and have faith in the word of God. If God said it; he would do what he says he will do on any situation/s big or small. "But without faith it is impossible to please him: for he that cometh to God must believe that he is, and that he is a rewarder of them that diligently seek Him." (He. 11:6 KJV) and God will do according to His word. "God is not a man, that He should lie; neither the Son of Man, that He should repent: hath He said, and shall He not do it? Or hath He spoken, and shall He not make it good?" (Nu. 23:19 KJV)

*Instructions:

In this manual you will have an understanding of the terms you may refer back to Webster's revised unabridged dictionary, Webster's new pocket dictionary, https://en.wikipedia.org, and reference scriptures from the Holy Bible (King James Version). One can use it while praying or communicating to God for yourself and others in the situation one may be faced with.

Books of the Bible And Abbreviations

Old Testament

Genesis, *Ge*	Ezra, *Ezr*	Joel, *Joel*
Exodus, *Ex*	Nehemiah, *Ne*	Amos, *Am*
Leviticus, *Le*	Ester, *Est*	Obadiah, *Obad*
Numbers, *Nu*	Job, *Jb*	Jonah, *Jona*
Deuteronomy, *De*	Psalms, *Ps*	Micah, *Mi*
Joshua, *Jos*	Proverbs, *Pr*	Nahum, *Na*
Judges, *Jud*	Ecclesiastes, *Ec*	Habakkuk, *Hab*
Ruth, *Ru*	Song of Solomon, *Song*	Zephaniah, *Zep*
1 Samuel, *1 S*	Isaiah, *Is*	Haggi, *Hag*
2 Samuel, *2 S*	Jeremiah, *Je*	Zechariah, *Zec*
1 Kings, *1 K*	Lamentations, *Lam*	Malachi, *Mal*
2 Kings, *2 K*	Ezekial, *Eze*	
1 Chronicles, *1 Chr*	Daniel, *Da*	
2 Chronicles, *2 Chr*	Hosea, *Ho*	

New Testament

Matthew, *Mt*	Philippians, *Ph*	1 Peter, *1 Pe*
Mark, *Mk*	Colossians, *Col*	2 Peter, *2 Pe*
Luke, *Lu*	1 Thessalonians, *1 Th*	1 John, *1 Jn*
John, *Jn*	2 Thessalonians, *2 Th*	2 John, *2 Jn*
Acts, *Ac*	1 Timothy, *1 Ti*	3 John, *3 Jn*
Romans, *Ro*	2 Timothy, *2 Ti*	Jude, *Jude*
1 Corinthians, *1 Co*	Titus, *Tit*	Revelations, *Re*
2 Corinthians, *2 Co*	Philemon, *Phm*	
Galatians, *Ga*	Hebrews, *He*	
Ephesians, *Ep*	James, *Ja*	

These Are Some Keys To
Living A Daily Victorious Life

- **Repentance:** "The act of turning around an improper behavior; sorrow for what one has done; especially, contrition for sin." (WRUD)

  ### SCRIPTURE READING:

  A. "I indeed baptize you with water unto repentance: but he that cometh after me is mightier than I, whose shoes I am not worthy to bear: he shall baptize you with the Holy Ghost, and with fire." (Mt. 3:11 KJV)

  B. "And that repentance and remission of sins should be preached in his name among all nations, beginning at Jerusalem." (Lu. 24:47 KJV)

  C. "Or despisest thou the riches of his goodness and forbearance and longsuffering; not knowing that the goodness of God leadeth thee to repentance?" (Ro. 2:4 KJV)

  D. "I say unto you, that likewise joy shall be in heaven over one sinner that repenteth, more than over ninety and nine just persons, which need no repentance." (Lu. 15:7 KJV)

  E. "The Lord is not slack concerning his promise, as some men count slackness; but is longsuffering to us-ward, not willing that any should perish, but that all should come to repentance." (2 Pe. 3:9 KJV)

- **Suffering:** "The bearing of pain, inconvenience, or loss; pain endured; distress, loss, or injury incurred; as, sufferings by pain or sorrow; sufferings by want or by wrongs, being in pain or grief; having loss, injury, distress, etc." (WRUD)

A. "But thou, O Lord, art a God full of compassion, and gracious, longsuffering, and plenteous in mercy and truth." (Ps. 86:15 KJV)

B. "O LORD, thou knowest: remember me, and visit me, and revenge me of my persecutors; take me not away in thy longsuffering: know that for thy sake I have suffered rebuke." (Je. 15:15 KJV)

C. "For Christ also hath once suffered for sins, the just for the unjust, that he might bring us to God, being put to death in the flesh, but quickened by the Spirit." (1 Pe. 3:18 KJV)

D. "And whether we be afflicted, it is for your consolation and salvation, which is effectual in the enduring of the same sufferings which we also suffer: or whether we be comforted, it is for your consolation and salvation." (2 Co. 1:6 KJV)

E. "But rejoice, inasmuch as ye are partakers of Christ's sufferings; that, when his glory shall be revealed, ye may be glad also with exceeding joy." (1 Pe. 4:13 KJV)

- *Fear:* "A painful emotion or passion excited by the expectation of evil, or the apprehension of impending danger; apprehension; anxiety; solicitude; alarm; dread." (WRUD)

SCRIPTURE READING:

A. "Only fear the LORD, and serve him in truth with all your heart: for consider how great things he hath done for you." (1 S. 12:24 KJV)

B. "Let us hear the conclusion of the whole matter: Fear God, and keep his commandments: for this is the whole duty of man." (Ec. 12:13 KJV)

C. "And wisdom and knowledge shall be the stability of thy times, and strength of salvation: the fear of the LORD is his treasure." (Is. 33:6 KJV)

D. "Yea, though I walk through the valley of the shadow of death, I will fear no evil: for thou art with me; thy rod and thy staff they comfort me." (Ps. 23:4 KJV)

E. "For ye have not received the spirit of bondage again to fear; but ye have received the Spirit of adoption, whereby we cry, Abba, Father." (Ro. 8:15 KJV)

- **_Prayer:_** "The act of addressing supplication to a divinity, especially to the true God; the offering of adoration, confession, supplication, and thanksgiving to the Supreme Being; as, public prayer; secret prayer." (WRUD)

  SCRIPTURE READING:

  A. "My voice shalt thou hear in the morning, O LORD; in the morning will I direct my prayer unto thee, and will look up." (Ps. 5:3 KJV)

  B. "The Lord hath heard my supplication; the Lord will receive my prayer." (Ps. 6:9 KJV)

  C. "And all things, whatsoever ye shall ask in prayer, believing, ye shall receive." (Mt. 21:22 KJV)

  D. "Rejoice in hope; patient in tribulation; continuing instant in prayer." (Ro. 12:12 KJV)

  E. "Be careful for nothing; but in everything by prayer and supplication with thanksgiving let your requests be made known unto God." (Ph. 4:6 KJV)

- **_Healing:_** "Tending to cure; soothing; mollifying; as, the healing art; a healing salve; healing words." (WRUD)

  SCRIPTURE READING:

  A. "He sent his word, and healed them, and delivered them from their destruction." (Ps. 107:20 KJV)

  B. "I said, Lord, be merciful unto me: heal my soul; for I have sinned against thee." (Ps. 41:4 KJV)

  C. "Heal me, O LORD, and I shall be healed; save me, and I shall be saved: for thou art my praise." (Je. 17:14 KJV)

  D. "But he was wounded for our transgressions; he was bruised for our iniquities: the chastisement of our peace was upon him; and with his stripes we are healed." (Is. 53:5 KJV)

E. "He healeth the broken in heart, and bindeth up their wounds." (Ps. 147:3 KJV)

- *Forgiveness:* "The act of forgiving; the state of being forgiven; as, the forgiveness of sin or of injuries." (WRUD)

SCRIPTURE READING:

A. "In whom we have redemption through his blood, even the forgiveness of sins." (Col. 1:14 KJV)

B. "For if ye forgive men their trespasses, your heavenly Father will also forgive you." (Mt. 6:14 KJV)

C. "And be ye kind one to another, tenderhearted, forgiving one another, even as God for Christ's sake hath forgiven you." (Ep. 4:32 KJV)

D. 25 "And when ye stand praying, forgive, if ye have ought against any: that your Father also which is in heaven may forgive you your trespasses." 26 "But if ye do not forgive, neither will your Father which is in heaven forgive your trespasses." (Mk. 11:25-26 KJV)

E. "Then said Jesus, Father, forgive them; for they know not what they do. And they parted his raiment, and cast lots." (Lu. 23:34 KJV)

- *Holy Spirit:* "In Judaism, the Holy Spirit is the divine force, quality, and influence of God over the Universe or over his creatures. In Nicene Christianity, the Holy Spirit or Holy Ghost is the third person of the Trinity. In Islam, the Holy Spirit acts as an agent of divine action or communication. In the Baha'i Faith, the Holy Spirit is seen as the intermediary between God and man and "the outpouring grace of God and the effulgent rays that emanate from His Manifestation." (Wik)

SCRIPTURE READING:

A. "Cast me not away from thy presence; and take not the Holy Spirit form me." (Ps. 51:11 KJV)

B. "In whom ye also trusted, after that ye heard the word of truth, the gospel of your salvation: in whom also after that ye believed, ye were sealed with that Holy Spirit of promise." (Ep. 1:13 KJV)

C. "The Spirit of the Lord is upon me, because he hath anointed me to preach the gospel to the poor; he hath sent me to heal the brokenhearted, to preach deliverance to the captives, and recovering of sight to the blind, to set at liberty them that are bruised." (Lu. 4:18 KJV)

D. "And they were all filled with the Holy Ghost, and began to speak with other tongues, as the Spirit gave them utterance." (Ac. 2:4 KJV)

E. "For the kingdom of God is not meat and drink; but righteousness, and peace, and joy in the Holy Ghost." (Ro. 14:17 KJV)

- *Evangelism:* "The preacher of the Gospel." (WNPD)

   SCRIPTURE READING:

   A. 19 "Go ye therefore, and teach all nations, baptizing them in the name of the Father, and of the Son, and of the Holy Ghost: 20 Teaching them to observe all things whatsoever I have commanded you: and, lo, I am with you always, even unto the end of the world. Amen." (Mt. 28:19-20 KJV)

   B. "No man can come to me, except the Father which hath sent me draw him: and I will raise him up at the last day." (Jn. 6:44 KJV)

   C. 18 "And all things are of God, who hath reconciled us to himself by Jesus Christ, and hath given to us the ministry of reconciliation; 19 To wit; that God was in Christ, reconciling the world unto himself, not imputing their trespasses unto them; and hath committed unto us the word of reconciliation. 20 Now then we are ambassadors for Christ, as though God did beseech you by us: we pray you in Christ's stead, be ye reconciled to God." (2 Co. 5:18-20 KV)

   D. 15 "And he said unto them, Go ye into all the world, and preach the gospel to every creature 16 He that believeth and is baptized shall be saved; but he that believeth not shall be damned. 17 And these signs shall follow them that believe; In my name shall they cast out devils; they shall speak with new tongues." (Mk. 16:15-17 KJV)

E. "For I neither received it of man, neither was I taught it, but by the revelation of Jesus Christ." (Ga. 1:12 KJV)

- *Doubt:* "To waver in opinion or judgment; to be in uncertainty as to belief respecting anything; to hesitate in belief; to be undecided as to the truth of the negative or the affirmative proposition; to be undetermined." (WRUD)

  SCRIPTURE READING:

  A. 21 "Jesus answered and said unto them, Verily I say unto you, If ye have faith, doubt not, ye shall not only do this which is done to the fig tree, but also if ye shall say unto this mountain, Be thou removed, and be thou cast into the sea; it shall be done. 22 And all things, whatsoever ye shall ask in prayer, believing, ye shall receive." (Mt. 21:21-22 KJV)

  B. "And seek not ye what ye eat, or what ye shall drink, neither be ye of doubtful mind." (Lu. 12:29 KJV)

  C. "And he that doubteth is damned if he eat, because he eateth not of faith: for whatsoever is not of faith is sin." (Ro. 14:23 KJV)

  D. "I will therefore that men pray every where, lifting up holy hands, without wrath and doubting." (1 Ti. 2:8 KJV)

  E. "But let him ask in faith, nothing wavering. For he that wavering is like a wave of the sea driven with the wind and tossed. For let not that man think that he shall receive any thing of the Lord. A double minded man is unstable in all his ways." (Ja. 1:6 KJV)

- *Marriage:* "The act of marrying, or the state of being married; legal union of a man and a woman for life, as husband and wife; wedlock; matrimony." (WRUD)

  SCRIPTURE READING:

  A. "And the LORD God said, It is not good that the man should be alone, I will make him an help meet for him." (Ge. 2:18 KJV)

  B. "Therefore shall a man leave his father and his mother, and shall cleave unto his wife: and they shall be one flesh." (Ge. 2:24 KJV)

    C. "Marriage is honorable in all, and the bed undefiled: but whoremongers and adulterers God will judge." (He. 13:4 KJV)

    D. "I will therefore that the younger women marry, bear children, guide the house, give none occasion to the adversary to speak reproachfully." (1 Ti. 5:14 KJV)

    E. "For thy Maker is thine husband; the LORD of hosts is his name; and thy Redeemer the Holy One of Israel; The God of the whole earth shall he be called." (Is. 54:5 KJV)

- *Hell:* "The place or state of punishment for the wicked after death; the abode of evil spirits. Hence, any mental torment; anguish." (WRUD)

    SCRIPTURE READINGS:

    A. "The wicked shall be turned into hell, and all the nations that forget God." (Ps. 9:17 KJV)

    B. "For great is thy mercy toward me: and thou hast delivered my soul from the lowest hell." (Ps. 86:13 KJV)

    C. "Hell and destruction are never full; so the eyes of man are never satisfied." (Pr. 27:20 KJV)

    D. "And said, I cried by reason of mine affliction unto the LORD, and he heard me; out of the belly of hell cried I, and thou heardest my voice." (Jona. 2:2 KJV)

    E. "And fear not them which kill the body, but are not able to kill the soul: but rather fear him which is able to destroy both soul and body in hell." (Mt. 10:28 KJV)

- *Divorce:* "A legal dissolution of the marriage contract by a court or other body having competent authority. This is properly a divorce, and called, technically, divorce a vinculo matrimonii." (WRUD)

    SCRIPTURE READING:

    A. 31 "It hath been said, Whosoever shall put away his wife, let him give her a writing of divorcement. 32 But I say unto you, That whosoever shall put away his wife, saving for the cause of fornication, causeth her to commit adultery: and whosoever shall marry her that is divorced committeth adultery." (Matt. 5:31-32 KJV)

B. "And if the latter husband hates her, and writes her a bill of divorcement, and giveth it in her hand, and sendeth her out of his house; or if the latter husband die, which took her to be his wife." (De. 24:3 KJV)

C. "What therefore God hath joined together, let not man put asunder." (Mk. 10:9 KJV)

D. "Whosoever putteth away his wife, and marrieth another, committeth adultery: and whosoever marrieth her that is put away from her husband committeth adultery." (Lu. 16:18 KJV)

E. "The wife is bound by the law as long as her husband liveth; but if her husband be dead, she is at liberty to be married to whom she will; only in the Lord." (1 Co. 7:39 KJV)

- *Loneliness:* "Being without a companion; being by one's self; also, sad from lack of companionship; lonely; as, a lone traveler or watcher." (WRUD)

    SCRIPTURE READING:

    A. "For the LORD will not forsake his people for his great name's sake: because it hath pleased the LORD to make you his people." (1 S. 12:22 KJV)

    B. "I sat not in the assembly of the mockers, nor rejoiced; I sat alone because of thy hand: for thou hast filled me with indignation." (Je. 15:17 KJV)

    C. "And Jacob was left alone; and there wrestled a man with him until the breaking of the day." (Ge. 32:24 KJV)

    D. "Let your conversation be without covetousness; and be content with such things as ye have: for he hath said, I will never leave thee, nor forsake thee." (He. 13:5 KJV)

    E. "When my father and my mother forsake me, then the LORD will take me up." (Ps. 27:10 KJV)

- *Courage:* "That quality of mind which enables one to encounter danger and difficulties with firmness, or without fear, or fainting of heart; valor; boldness; resolution." (WRUD)

A. "Be strong and of good courage, do not fear nor be afraid of them; for the Lord your God, He is the One who goes with you. He will not leave you not forsake you." (De. 31:6 KJV)

B. "The Lord is my light and my salvation- whom shall I fear? The Lord is the stronghold of my life- of whom shall I be afraid?" (Ps. 27:1 KJV)

C. 3 "What time I am afraid, I will trust in thee. 4 In God I will praise his word, in God I have put my trust; I will not fear what flesh can do unto me." (Ps. 56:3-4 KJV)

D. "Fear thou not; for I am with thee: be not dismayed; for I am thy God: I will strengthen thee; yea, I will help thee; yea, I will uphold thee with the right hand of my righteousness." (Is. 41:10 KJV)

E. "For I the LORD thy God will hold thy right hand, saying unto thee, Fear not; I will help thee." (Is. 41:13 KJV)

- *Comfort:* "To impart strength and hope to; to encourage; to relieve; to console; to cheer." (WRUD)

A. "Ye shall not fear them: for the LORD your God he shall fight for you." (De. 3:22 KJV)

B. "The LORD is my light and my salvation; whom shall I fear? the LORD is the strength of my life; of whom shall I be afraid?" (Ps. 27:1 KJV)

C. "Give me a sign of your goodness, that my enemies may see it and be put to shame, for you, Lord, have helped me and comforted me." (Ps. 86:17 KJV)

D. "When thou liest down, thou shalt not be afraid: yea, thou shalt lie down, and thy sleep shall be sweet." (Pr. 3:24 KJV)

E. "Be not afraid of their faces: for I am with thee to deliver thee, saith the LORD." (Je. 1:8 KJV)

- *Hope:* "A desire of some good, accompanied with an expectation of obtaining it, or a belief that it is obtainable; an expectation of something which is thought to be desirable; confidence; pleasing expectancy." (WRUD)

A. "But they that wait upon the LORD shall renew their strength; they shall mount up with wings as eagles; they shall run, and not be weary; and they shall walk, and not faint." (Is. 40:31 KJV)

B. "To whom God would make known what is the riches of the glory of this mystery among the Gentiles; which is Christ in you, the hope of glory." (Col. 1:27 KJV)

C. "God is not a man, that he should lie; neither the son of man, that he should repent: hath he said, and shall he not do it? or hath he spoken, and shall he not make it good?" (Nu. 23:19 KJV)

D. "Now faith is the substance of things hoped for, the evidence of things not seen. For by it the elders obtained a good report." (He. 11:1 KJV)

E. "Now the God of hope fill you with all joy and peace in believing, that ye may abound in hope, through the power of the Holy Ghost." (Ro. 15:13 KJV)

- *Joy:* "The passion or emotion excited by the acquisition or expectation of good; pleasurable feelings or emotions caused by success, good fortune, and the like, or by a rational prospect of possessing what we love or desire; gladness; exhilaration of spirits; delight." (WRUD)

A. 1 "O clap your hands, all ye people; shout unto God with the voice of triumph. 2 For the LORD most high is terrible; he is a great King over all the earth. 3 He shall subdue the people under us, and the nations under our feet." (Ps. 47:1-3 KJV)

B. "My lips shall greatly rejoice when I sing unto thee; and my soul, which thou hast redeemed." (Ps. 71:23 KJV)

C. "The hope of the righteous shall be gladness: but the expectation of the wicked shall perish." (Pr. 10:28 KJV)

D. 1 "Paul and Timotheus, the servants of Jesus Christ, to all the saints in Christ Jesus which are at Philippi, with the bishops and deacons: 2 Grace be unto you, and peace, from God our Father, and from the Lord Jesus Christ. 3 I thank my God upon every remembrance of you, 4 Always in every prayer of mine for you all making request with joy, 5 For your fellowship in the gospel from the first day until now." (Ph. 1:3-5 KJV)

E. "For we have great joy and consolation in thy love, because the bowels of the saints are refreshed by thee, brother." (Phm. 1:7 KJV)

- *Thankfulness:* "Impressed with a sense of kindness received, and ready to acknowledge it; grateful." (WRUD)

SCRIPTURE READING:

A. "O give thanks unto the LORD; for he is good; for his mercy endureth forever." (1 Chr. 16:34 KJV)

B. "The LORD is my strength and my shield; my heart trusted in him, and I am helped: therefore my heart greatly rejoiceth; and with my song will I praise him." (Ps. 28:7 KJV)

C. "Enter into his gates with thanksgiving, and into his courts with praise: be thankful unto him, and bless his name." (Ps. 100:4 KJV)

D. "Praise ye the LORD. O give thanks unto the LORD; for he is good: for his mercy endureth forever." (Ps. 106:1 KJV)

E. 28 "Wherefore we receiving a kingdom which cannot be moved, let us have grace, whereby we may serve God acceptably with reverence and godly fear: 29 For our God is a consuming fire." (He. 12:28-29 KJV)

- *Sin:* "Transgression of the law of God; disobedience of the divine command; any violation of God's will, either in purpose or conduct; moral deficiency in the character; iniquity; as, sins of omission and sins of commission." (WRUD)

SCRIPTURE READING:

A. "For this is my blood of the new testament, which is shed for many for the remission of sins." (Mt. 26:28 KJV)

B. "The next day John seeth Jesus coming unto him, and saith, Behold the Lamb of God, which taketh away the sin of the world," (Jn. 1:29 KJV)

C. 28 "And even as they did not like to retain God in their knowledge, God gave them over to a reprobate mind, to do those things which are not convenient; 29 "Being filled with all unrighteousness, fornication, wickedness, covetousness, maliciousness; full of envy, murder, debate, deceit, malignity; whisperers, 30 Backbiters, haters of God, despiteful, proud, boasters, inventors of evil things, disobedient to parents, 31 Without understanding, covenantbreakers, without natural affection, implacable, unmerciful: 32 Who knowing the judgment of God, that they which commit such things are worthy of death, not only do the same, but have pleasure in them that do them." (Ro. 1:28-32 KJV)

D. 20 "Moreover the law entered, that the offence might abound. But where sin abounded, grace did much more abound: 21That as sin hath reigned unto death, even so might grace reign through righteousness unto eternal life by Jesus Christ our Lord." (Ro. 5:20-21 KJV)

E. 9 "But ye are not in the flesh, but in the Spirit, if so be that the Spirit of God dwell in you. Now if any man have not the Spirit of Christ, he is none of his. 10 And if Christ be in you, the body is dead because of sin; but the Spirit is life because of righteousness. 11 But if the Spirit of him that raised up Jesus from the dead dwell in you, he that raised up Christ from the dead shall also quicken your mortal bodies by his Spirit that dwelleth in you." (Ro. 8:9-11 KJV)

- *Trust:* "To place confidence in; to rely on, to confide, or repose faith, in; as, we can not trust those who have deceived us." (WRUD)

SCRIPTURE READING:

A. 12 "But as many as received him, to them gave he power to become the sons of God, even to them that believe on his name: 13 Which were born, not of blood, nor of the will of the flesh, nor of the will of man, but of God." (Jn. 1:12-13 KJV)

B. "He that believeth on him is not condemned: but he that believeth not is condemned already, because he hath not believed in the name of the only begotten Son of God." (Jn. 3:18 KJV)

Books of the Bible And Abbreviations

Old Testament

Genesis, *Ge*

Exodus, *Ex*

Leviticus, *Le*

Numbers, *Nu*

Deuteronomy, *De*

Joshua, *Jos*

Judges, *Jud*

Ruth, *Ru*

1 Samuel, *1 S*

2 Samuel, *2 S*

1 Kings, *1 K*

2 Kings, *2 K*

1 Chronicles, *1 Chr*

2 Chronicles, *2 Chr*

Ezra, *Ezr*

Nehemiah, *Ne*

Ester, *Est*

Job, *Jb*

Psalms, *Ps*

Proverbs, *Pr*

Ecclesiastes, *Ec*

Song of Solomon, *Song*

Isaiah, *Is*

Jeremiah, *Je*

Lamentations, *Lam*

Ezekial, *Eze*

Daniel, *Da*

Hosea, *Ho*

Joel, *Joel*

Amos, *Am*

Obadiah, *Obad*

Jonah, *Jona*

Micah, *Mi*

Nahum, *Na*

Habakkuk, *Hab*

Zephaniah, *Zep*

Haggi, *Hag*

Zechariah, *Zec*

Malachi, *Mal*

New Testament

Matthew, *Mt*

Mark, *Mk*

Luke, *Lu*

John, *Jn*

Acts, *Ac*

Romans, *Ro*

1 Corinthians, *1 Co*

2 Corinthians, *2 Co*

Galatians, *Ga*

Ephesians, *Ep*

Philippians, *Ph*

Colossians, *Col*

1 Thessalonians, *1 Th*

2 Thessalonians, *2 Th*

1 Timothy, *1 Ti*

2 Timothy, *2 Ti*

Titus, *Tit*

Philemon, *Phm*

Hebrews, *He*

James, *Ja*

1 Peter, *1 Pe*

2 Peter, *2 Pe*

1 John, *1 Jn*

2 John, *2 Jn*

3 John, *3 Jn*

Jude, *Jude*

Revelations, *Re*

C. "Now the God of hope fill you with all joy and peace in believing, that ye may abound in hope, through the power of the Holy Ghost." (Ro. 15:13 KJV)

D. "But as we were allowed of God to be put in trust with the gospel, even so we speak; not as pleasing men, but God, which trieth our hearts." (1 Th. 2:4 KJV)

E. "For therefore we both labour and suffer reproach, because we trust in the living God, who is the Saviour of all men, specially of those that believe." (1 Ti. 4:10 KJV)

- *Reconciliation:* "The act of reconciling, or the state of being reconciled; reconcilement; restoration to harmony; renewal of friendship." (WRUD)

SCRIPTURE READING:

A. 10 "For if, when we were enemies, we were reconciled to God by the death of his Son, much more, being reconciled, we shall be saved by his life. 11 And not only so, but we also joy in God through our Lord Jesus Christ, by whom we have now received the atonement." (Ro. 5:10-11 KJV)

B. "For if the casting away of them be the reconciling of the world, what shall the receiving of them be, but life from the dead?" (Ro. 11:15 KJV)

C. 17 "Therefore if any man be in Christ, he is a new creature: old things are passed away; behold, all things are become new. 18 And all things are of God, who hath reconciled us to himself by Jesus Christ, and hath given to us the ministry of reconciliation; 19 To wit, that God was in Christ, reconciling the world unto himself, not imputing their trespasses unto them; and hath committed unto us the word of reconciliation. 20 Now then we are ambassadors for Christ, as though God did beseech you by us: we pray you in Christ's stead, be ye reconciled to God." (2 Co. 5:17-20 KJV)

D. "Wherefore in all things it behoved him to be made like unto his brethren, that he might be a merciful and faithful high priest in things pertaining to God, to make reconciliation for the sins of the people." (He. 2:17 KJV)

E. "Seventy weeks are determined upon thy people and upon thy holy city, to finish the transgression, and to make an end of sins, and to make reconciliation for iniquity, and to bring in everlasting righteousness, and to seal up the vision and prophecy, and to anoint the most Holy." (Da. 9:24 KJV)

- *Transgression:* "The act of transgressing, or of passing over or beyond any law, civil or moral; the violation of a law or known principle of rectitude; breach of command; fault; offense; crime; sin." (WRUD)

SCRIPTURE READING:

A. "Because the law worketh wrath: for where no law is, there is no transgression." (Ro. 4:15 KJV)

B. 14 "Nevertheless death reigned from Adam to Moses, even over them that had not sinned after the similitude of Adam's transgression, who is the figure of him that was to come. 15 But not as the offence, so also is the free gift. For if through the offence of one many be dead, much more the grace of God, and the gift by grace, which is by one man, Jesus Christ, hath abounded unto many. 16 And not as it was by one that sinned, so is the gift: for the judgment was by one to condemnation, but the free gift is of many offences unto justification. 17 For if by one man's offence death reigned by one; much more they which receive abundance of grace and of the gift of righteousness shall reign in life by one, Jesus Christ.) 18 Therefore as by the offence of one judgment came upon all men to condemnation; even so by the righteousness of one the free gift came upon all men unto justification of life. 19 For as by one man's disobedience many were made sinners, so by the obedience of one shall many be made righteous. 20 Moreover the law entered, that the offence might abound. But where sin abounded, grace did much more abound: 21 That as sin hath reigned unto death, even so might grace reign through righteousness unto eternal life by Jesus Christ our Lord." (Ro. 5:14-21 KJV)

C. "Whosoever committeth sin transgresseth also the law: for sin is the transgression of the law." (1 Jn. 3:4 KJV)

D. "But he was wounded for our transgressions, he was bruised for our iniquities: the chastisement of our peace was upon him; and with his stripes we are healed." (Is. 53:3 KJV)

E. "The desire of the righteous is only good: but the expectation of the wicked is wrath." (Pr. 11:23 KJV)

- *Surrender:* "The act of surrendering; the act of yielding, or resigning one's person, or the possession of something, into the power of another; as, the surrender of a castle to an enemy; the surrender of a right." (WRUD)

SCRIPTURE READING:

A. "Neither yield ye your members as instruments of unrighteousness unto sin: but yield yourselves unto God, as those that are alive from the dead, and your members as instruments of righteousness unto God." (Ro. 6:13 KJV)

B. "Know ye not, that to whom ye yield yourselves servants to obey, his servants ye are to whom ye obey; whether of sin unto death, or of obedience unto righteousness?" (Ro. 6:16 KJV)

C. "And though I bestow all my goods to feed the poor, and though I give my body to be burned, and have not charity, it profiteth me nothing." (1 Co. 13:3 KJV)

D. "Then cometh the end, when he shall have delivered up the kingdom to God, even the Father; when he shall have put down all rule and all authority and power." (1 Co. 15:24 KJV)

E. "The LORD will preserve him, and keep him alive; and he shall be blessed upon the earth: and thou wilt not deliver him unto the will of his enemies." (Ps. 41:2 KJV)

- *Gift:* "Some quality or endowment given to man by God; a preeminent and special talent or aptitude; power; faculty; as, the gift of wit; a gift for speaking." (WRUD)

SCRIPTURE READING:

A. "For the wages of sin is death; but the gift of God is eternal life through Jesus Christ our Lord." (Ro. 6:23 KJV)

B. 4 "Now there are diversities of gifts, but the same Spirit. 5 And there are differences of administrations, but the same Lord. 6 And there are diversities of operations, but it is the same God which worketh all in all. 7 But the manifestation of the Spirit is given to every man to profit withal. 8 For to one is given by the Spirit the word of wisdom; to another the word of knowledge by the same Spirit; 9 To another faith by the same Spirit; to another the gifts of healing by the same Spirit; 10 To another the working of miracles; to another prophecy; to another discerning of spirits; to another divers kinds of tongues; to another the interpretation of tongues: 11 But all these worketh that one and the selfsame Spirit, dividing to every man severally as he will." (1 Co. 12:4-11 KJV)

C. "Praying us with much intreaty that we would receive the gift, and take upon us the fellowship of the ministering to the saints." (2 Co. 8:4 KJV)

D. "Thanks be unto God for his unspeakable gift." (2 Co. 9:15 KJV)

E. "Every good gift and every perfect gift is from above, and cometh down from the Father of lights, with whom is no variableness, neither shadow of turning." (Ja. 1:17 KJV)

- *Faith:* "The belief in the facts and truth of the Scriptures, with a practical love of them; especially, that confiding and affectionate belief in the person and work of Christ, which affects the character and life, and makes a man a true Christian, -- called a practical, evangelical, or saving faith." (WRUD)

SCRIPTURE READING:

A. 23 "For verily I say unto you, That whosoever shall say unto this mountain, Be thou removed, and be thou cast into the sea; and shall not doubt in his heart, but shall believe that those things which he saith shall come to pass; he shall have whatsoever he saith. 24 Therefore I say unto you, What things soever ye desire, when ye pray, believe that ye receive them, and ye shall have them." (Mk. 11:23-24 KJV)

B. 16 "He that believeth and is baptized shall be saved; but he that believeth not shall be damned. 17 And these signs shall follow them that believe; In my name shall they cast out devils; they shall speak with new tongues; 18 They shall take up serpents; and if they drink any deadly thing, it shall not hurt them; they shall lay hands on the sick, and they shall recover." (Mk. 16:16-18 KJV)

C. "But I have prayed for thee, that thy faith fail not: and when thou art converted, strengthen thy brethren." (Lu. 22:32 KJV)

D. 15 "That whosoever believeth in him should not perish, but have eternal life. 16 For God so loved the world, that he gave his only begotten Son, that whosoever believeth in him should not perish, but have everlasting life. 17 For God sent not his Son into the world to condemn the world; but that the world through him might be saved. 18 He that believeth on him is not condemned: but he that believeth not is condemned already, because he hath not believed in the name of the only begotten Son of God." (Jn. 3:15-18 KJV)

E. "Verily, verily, I say unto you, He that believeth on me hath everlasting life." (Jn. 6:47 KJV)

- *Love:* "A feeling of strong attachment induced by that which delights or commands admiration; preeminent kindness or devotion to another; affection; tenderness; as, the love of brothers and sisters." (WRUD)

SCRIPTURE READING:

A. 27 "And last of all the woman died also. 28 Therefore in the resurrection whose wife shall she be of the seven? for they all had her. 29 Jesus answered and said unto them, Ye do err, not knowing the scriptures, nor the power of God." (Mat. 22:27-29 KJV)

B. "No servant can serve two masters: for either he will hate the one, and love the other; or else he will hold to the one, and despise the other. Ye cannot serve God and mammon." (Lu. 16:13 KJV)

C. "For God so loved the world, that he gave his only begotten Son, that whosoever believeth in him should not perish, but have everlasting life." (Jn. 3:16 KJV)

D. "But God commendeth his love toward us, in that, while we were yet sinners, Christ died for us." (Ro. 5:8 KJV)

E. "And we know that all things work together for good to them that love God, to them who are the called according to his purpose." (Ro. 8:28 KJV)

- *Receive:* "To take, as something that is offered, given, committed, sent, paid, or the like; to accept; as, to receive money offered in payment of a debt; to receive a gift, a message, or a letter." (WRUD)

SCRIPTURE READING:

A. "For every one that asketh receiveth; and he that seeketh findeth; and to him that knocketh it shall be opened." (Mt. 7:8 KJV)

B. 38 "And he that taketh not his cross, and followeth after me, is not worthy of me. 39 He that findeth his life shall lose it: and he that loseth his life for my sake shall find it. 40 He that receiveth you receiveth me, and he that receiveth me receiveth him that sent me. 41 He that receiveth a prophet in the name of a prophet shall receive a prophet's reward; and he that receiveth a righteous man in the name of a righteous man shall receive a righteous man's reward." (Mt. 10:38-41 KJV)

C. "Verily I say unto you, Whosoever shall not receive the kingdom of God as a little child shall in no wise enter therein." (Lu. 18:17 KJV)

D. 9 "That was the true Light, which lighteth every man that cometh into the world. 10 He was in the world, and the world was made by him, and the world knew him not. 11 He came unto his own, and his own received him not. 12 But as many as received him, to them gave he power to become the sons of God, even to them that believe on his name: 13 Which were born, not of blood, nor of the will of the flesh, nor of the will of man, but of God." (Jn. 1:9-13 KJV)

E. 8 "But ye shall receive power, after that the Holy Ghost is come upon you: and ye shall be witnesses unto me both in Jerusalem, and in all Judaea, and in Samaria, and unto the uttermost part of the earth. 9 And when he had spoken these things, while they beheld, he was taken up; and a cloud received him out of their sight." (Ac. 1:8-9 KJV)

- *Commandment:* "An order or injunction given by authority; a command; a charge; a precept; a mandate." (WRUD)

SCRIPTURE READING:

A. 6 "I am the LORD thy God, which brought thee out of the land of Egypt, from the house of bondage. 7 Thou shalt have none other gods before me. 8 Thou shalt not make thee any graven image, or any likeness of any thing that is in heaven above, or that is in the earth beneath, or that is in the waters beneath the earth: 9 Thou shalt not bow down thyself unto them, nor serve them: for I the LORD thy God am a jealous God, visiting the iniquity of the fathers upon the children unto the third and fourth generation of them that hate me, 10 And shewing mercy unto thousands of them that love me and keep my commandments. 11 Thou shalt not take the name of the LORD thy God in vain: for the LORD will not hold him guiltless that taketh his name in vain. 12 Keep the sabbath day to sanctify it, as the LORD thy God hath commanded thee. 13 Six days thou shalt labour, and do all thy work: 14 But the seventh day is the sabbath of the LORD thy God: in it thou shalt not do any work, thou, nor thy son, nor thy daughter, nor thy manservant, nor thy maidservant, nor thine ox, nor thine ass, nor any of thy cattle, nor thy stranger that is within thy gates; that thy manservant and thy maidservant may rest as well as thou. 15 And remember that thou wast a servant in the land of Egypt, and that the LORD thy God brought thee out thence through a mighty hand and by a stretched out arm: therefore the LORD thy God commanded thee to keep the sabbath day. 16 Honour thy father and thy mother, as the LORD thy God hath commanded thee; that thy days may be prolonged, and that it may go well with thee, in the land which the LORD thy God giveth thee. 17 Thou shalt not kill. 18 Neither shalt thou commit adultery. 19 Neither shalt thou steal. 20 Neither shalt thou bear false witness against thy neighbour. 21 Neither shalt thou desire thy neighbour's wife, neither shalt thou covet thy neighbour's house, his field, or his manservant, or his maidservant, his ox, or his ass, or any thing that is thy neighbour's." (De. 5:6-21 KJV)

B. 11 "But thou, O man of God, flee these things; and follow after righteousness, godliness, faith, love, patience, meekness. 12 Fight the good fight of faith, lay hold on eternal life, whereunto thou art also called, and hast professed a good profession before many witnesses. 13 I give thee charge in the sight of God, who quickeneth all things, and before Christ Jesus, who before Pontius Pilate witnessed a good confession; 14 That thou keep this commandment without spot, unrebukeable, until the appearing of our Lord Jesus Christ: 15 Which in his times he shall shew, who is the blessed and only Potentate, the King of kings, and Lord of lords; 16 Who only hath immortality, dwelling in the light which no man can approach unto; whom no man hath seen, nor can see: to whom be honour and power everlasting. Amen." (1 Ti. 6:11-16 KJV)

C. 25 "Now to him that is of power to stablish you according to my gospel, and the preaching of Jesus Christ, according to the revelation of the mystery, which was kept secret since the world began, 26 But now is made manifest, and by the scriptures of the prophets, according to the commandment of the everlasting God, made known to all nations for the obedience of faith: 27 To God only wise, be glory through Jesus Christ for ever. Amen." (Ro. 16:25-27 KJV)

D. "If any man think himself to be a prophet, or spiritual, let him acknowledge that the things that I write unto you are the commandments of the Lord." (1 Co. 14:37 KJV)

E. 22 "And whatsoever we ask, we receive of him, because we keep his commandments, and do those things that are pleasing in his sight. 23 And this is his commandment, That we should believe on the name of his Son Jesus Christ, and love one another, as he gave us commandment. 24 And he that keepeth his commandments dwelleth in him, and he in him. And hereby we know that he abideth in us, by the Spirit which he hath given us." (1 Jn. 3:22-24 KJV)

- **Grace:** "The divine favor toward man; the mercy of God, as distinguished from His justice; also, any benefits His mercy imparts; divine love or pardon; a state of acceptance with God; enjoyment of the divine favor." (WRUD)

  SCRIPTURE READING:

  A. 14 "And the Word was made flesh, and dwelt among us, (and we beheld his glory, the glory as of the only begotten of the Father,) full of grace and truth. 15 John bare witness of him, and cried, saying, This was he of whom I spake, He that cometh after me is preferred before me: for he was before me. 16 And of his fulness have all we received, and grace for grace. 17 For the law was given by Moses, but grace and truth came by Jesus Christ." (Jn. 1:14-17 KJV)

  B. "But we believe that through the grace of the Lord Jesus Christ we shall be saved, even as they." (Ac. 15:11 KJV)

  C. 24 "Being justified freely by his grace through the redemption that is in Christ Jesus: 25 Whom God hath set forth to be a propitiation through faith in his blood, to declare his righteousness for the remission of sins that are past, through the forbearance of God; 26 To declare, I say, at this time his righteousness: that he might be just, and the justifier of him which believeth in Jesus." (Ro. 3:24-26 KJV)

  D. 14 "For sin shall not have dominion over you: for ye are not under the law, but under grace. 15 What then? shall we sin, because we are not under the law, but under grace? God forbid." (Ro. 6:14-15 KJV)

  E. 8 "For by grace are ye saved through faith; and that not of yourselves: it is the gift of God: 9 Not of works, lest any man should boast." (Ep. 2:8-9 KJV)

- **Mercy:** "Compassionate treatment of the unfortunate and helpless; sometimes, favor, beneficence." (WRUD)

  SCRIPTURE READING:

  A. "Blessed are the merciful: for they shall obtain mercy." (Mt. 5:7 KJV)

B. "But go ye and learn what that meaneth, I will have mercy, and not sacrifice: for I am not come to call the righteous, but sinners to repentance." (Mt. 9:13 KJV)

C. "And his mercy is on them that fear him from generation to generation." (Lu. 1:50 KJV)

D. 25 "Whom God hath set forth to be a propitiation through faith in his blood, to declare his righteousness for the remission of sins that are past, through the forbearance of God; 26 To declare, I say, at this time his righteousness: that he might be just, and the justifier of him which believeth in Jesus." (Ro. 3:25-26 KJV)

E. 15 "For he saith to Moses, I will have mercy on whom I will have mercy, and I will have compassion on whom I will have compassion. 16 So then it is not of him that willeth, nor of him that runneth, but of God that sheweth mercy. 17 For the scripture saith unto Pharaoh, Even for this same purpose have I raised thee up, that I might shew my power in thee, and that my name might be declared throughout all the earth. 18 Therefore hath he mercy on whom he will have mercy, and whom he will he hardeneth." (Ro. 9:15-18 KJV)

- *Salvation:* "The redemption of man from the bondage of sin and liability to eternal death, and the conferring on him of everlasting happiness." (WRUD)

SCRIPTURE READING:

A. "And all flesh shall see the salvation of God." (Lu. 3:6 KJV)

B. "For godly sorrow worketh repentance to salvation not to be repented of: but the sorrow of the world worketh death." (2 Co. 7:10 KJV)

C. "And it shall come to pass, that whosoever shall call on the name of the Lord shall be saved." (Ac. 2:21 KJV)

D. "Neither is there salvation in any other: for there is none other name under heaven given among men, whereby we must be saved." (Ac. 4:12 KJV)

E. "For I am not ashamed of the gospel of Christ: for it is the power of God unto salvation to every one that believeth; to the Jew first, and also to the Greek." (Ro. 1:16 KJV)

- *Heaven:* "The sovereign of heaven; God; also, the assembly of the blessed, collectively; -- used variously in this sense, the dwelling place of the Deity; the abode of bliss; the place or state of the blessed after death." (WRUD)

    SCRIPTURE READING:

    A. "And saying, Repent ye: for the kingdom of heaven is at hand." (Mt. 3:2 KJV)

    B. "Blessed are the poor in spirit: for theirs is the kingdom of heaven." (Mt. 5:3 KJV)

    C. 14 "For if ye forgive men their trespasses, your heavenly Father will also forgive you: 15 But if ye forgive not men their trespasses, neither will your Father forgive your trespasses." (Mt. 6:14-15 KJV)

    D. 31 "Heaven and earth shall pass away: but my words shall not pass away. 32 But of that day and that hour knoweth no man, no, not the angels which are in heaven, neither the Son, but the Father." (Mk. 13:31-32 KJV)

    E. "Even so it is not the will of your Father which is in heaven, that one of these little ones should perish." (Mt. 18:14 KJV)

- *Inheritance:* "A permanent or valuable possession or blessing, esp. one received by gift or without purchase; a benefaction." (WRUD)

    SCRIPTURE READING:

    A. "And every one that hath forsaken houses, or brethren, or sisters, or father, or mother, or wife, or children, or lands, for my name's sake, shall receive an hundredfold, and shall inherit everlasting life." (Mt. 19:29 KJV)

    B. "To open their eyes, and to turn them from darkness to light, and from the power of Satan unto God, that they may receive forgiveness of sins, and inheritance among them which are sanctified by faith that is in me." (Ac. 26:18 KJV)

    C. 11 "In whom also we have obtained an inheritance, being predestinated according to the purpose of him who worketh all things after the counsel of his own will: 12 That we should be to the praise of his glory, who first trusted in Christ. 13 In whom ye also trusted, after that ye heard the word of truth, the gospel of your salvation: in whom also after that ye believed, ye were sealed with that holy Spirit of promise, 14 Which is the earnest of our inheritance until the redemption of the purchased possession, unto the praise of his glory." (Ep. 1:11-14 KJV)

D. 22 "Servants, obey in all things your masters according to the flesh; not with eyeservice, as menpleasers; but in singleness of heart, fearing God: 23 And whatsoever ye do, do it heartily, as to the Lord, and not unto men; 24 Knowing that of the Lord ye shall receive the reward of the inheritance: for ye serve the Lord Christ. 25 But he that doeth wrong shall receive for the wrong which he hath done: and there is no respect of persons." (Col. 3:22-25 KJV)

E. 3 "Blessed be the God and Father of our Lord Jesus Christ, which according to his abundant mercy hath begotten us again unto a lively hope by the resurrection of Jesus Christ from the dead, 4 To an inheritance incorruptible, and undefiled, and that fadeth not away, reserved in heaven for you, 5 Who are kept by the power of God through faith unto salvation ready to be revealed in the last time." (1 Pe. 1:3-5 KJV)

- *Holiness:* "The state or quality of being holy; perfect moral integrity or purity; freedom from sin; sanctity; innocence." (WRUD)

SCRIPTURE READING:

A. "But now being made free from sin, and become servants to God, ye have your fruit unto holiness, and the end everlasting life." (Ro. 6:22 KJV)

B. 30 "But of him are ye in Christ Jesus, who of God is made unto us wisdom, and righteousness, and sanctification, and redemption: 31 That, according as it is written, He that glorieth, let him glory in the Lord." (1 Co. 1:30-31 LKV)

C. "And that ye put on the new man, which after God is created in righteousness and true holiness." (Ep. 4:24 KJV)

D. 11 "Now God himself and our Father, and our Lord Jesus Christ, direct our way unto you. 12 And the Lord make you to increase and abound in love one toward another, and toward all men, even as we do toward you: 13 To the end he may stablish your hearts unblameable in holiness before God, even our Father, at the coming of our Lord Jesus Christ with all his saints." (1 Th. 3:11-13 KJV)

E. 2 "For ye know what commandments we gave you by the Lord Jesus. 3 For this is the will of God, even your sanctification, that ye should abstain from fornication: 4 That every one of you should know how to possess his vessel in sanctification and honour; 5 Not in the lust of concupiscence, even as the Gentiles which know not God: 6 That no man go beyond and defraud his brother in any matter: because that the Lord is the avenger of all such, as we also have forewarned you and testified. 7 For God hath not called us unto uncleanness, but unto holiness. 8 He therefore that despiseth, despiseth not man, but God, who hath also given unto us his holy Spirit." (1 Th. 4:2-8 KJV)

- **_Conversion:_** "A spiritual and moral change attending a change of belief with conviction; a change of heart; a change from the service of the world to the service of God; a change of the ruling disposition of the soul, involving a transformation of the outward life." (WRUD)

SCRIPTURE READING:

A. 19 "Repent ye therefore, and be converted, that your sins may be blotted out, when the times of refreshing shall come from the presence of the Lord; 20 And he shall send Jesus Christ, which before was preached unto you: 21 Whom the heaven must receive until the times of restitution of all things, which God hath spoken by the mouth of all his holy prophets since the world began. 22 For Moses truly said unto the fathers, A prophet shall the Lord your God raise up unto you of your brethren, like unto me; him shall ye hear in all things whatsoever he shall say unto you." (Ac. 3:19-22 KJV)

B. "For this people's heart is waxed gross, and their ears are dull of hearing, and their eyes they have closed; lest at any time they should see with their eyes, and hear with their ears, and should understand with their heart, and should be converted, and I should heal them." (Mt. 13:15 KJV)

C. "And said, Verily I say unto you, Except ye be converted, and become as little children, ye shall not enter into the kingdom of heaven." (Mt. 18:3 KJV)

D. 11 "And he said unto them, Unto you it is given to know the mystery of the kingdom of God: but unto them that are without, all these things are done in parables: 12 That seeing they may see, and not perceive; and hearing they may hear, and not understand; lest at any time they should be converted, and their sins should be forgiven them." (Mk. 4:11-12 KJV)

E. 3 "And being brought on their way by the church, they passed through Phenice and Samaria, declaring the conversion of the Gentiles: and they caused great joy unto all the brethren. 4 And when they were come to Jerusalem, they were received of the church, and of the apostles and elders, and they declared all things that God had done with them." (Ac. 15:3-4 KJV)

⁓ A Prayer ⁓

Father, I come to you in the name of the Lord Jesus Christ; I pray that the person who is using this manual for assistance in their life be touched by your presence. Lord, I command everything in their life to line up with the will of GOD. I speak the Blood of Jesus to cover them now in the name of Jesus. I ask that if this person is lost Lord, you will draw them to a place of repentance. I ask you Lord to build up their faith so they can believe/trust you for whatever is needed. Lord give he/she a heart to receive what you have for them this day. I pray that his/her journey in life will be as you created it. I stand on (Je. 29:11 KJV) "For I know the thoughts that I think toward you, saith the LORD, thoughts of peace, and not of evil, to give you an expected end." Also, (De. 28:2 KJV) "And all these blessings shall come on thee, and overtake thee if thou shalt hearken unto the voice of the LORD thy God." I know LORD you hear my prayer for this person because (Lam. 3:25 KJV) says; "The LORD is good to those who wait for Him, To the soul who seeks Him." I thank You for the new relationship that he/she now has with you LORD because they are seeking You for guidance in their life. Now, LORD, I thank you in advance for the blessings that you will release to this person. Hallelujah! I pray this prayer in the name of the Lord Jesus Christ. Amen.

Prophetic Release

"If my people, which are called by my name, shall humble themselves, and pray, and seek my face, and turn from their wicked ways; then will I hear from heaven, and will forgive their sin, and will heal their land." (2 Chr. 7:14 KJV) Now that you have come into the proper relationship with the Lord Jesus Christ; you have access to the Kingdom of GOD. Continue to build your relationship with the Lord Jesus Christ by seeking him for direction, wisdom, knowledge, understanding, clarification, and revelation through the Word of GOD with prayer and praise. Praise is a requirement; "Blessed be God, which hath not turned away my prayer, nor his mercy from me." (Ps. 66:20 KJV) "Be still and know that I am God: I will be exalted among the heathen, I will be exalted in the earth." (Ps. 46:10 KJV) Remember this one thing; "For it is written, As I live, saith the Lord, every knee shall bow to me, and every tongue shall confess to God." (Ro. 14:11 KJV) and have assurance to know that; "Howbeit when he, the Spirit of truth, is come, he will guide you into all truth: for he shall not speak of himself; but whatsoever he shall hear, that shall he speak: and he will shew you things to come." (Jn. 16:13 KJV) Amen!

Now that you are using the keys

and God has opened the door,

Just take one step by faith at a time.

Now you're walking into the open doors,

Embrace your new destiny!

Made in the USA
Columbia, SC
13 February 2024

31447712R00024

31447739R00024